iPhone

7 and 7 Plus

A Detailed and Easy-to-Use iPhone 7 and 7 Plus Book Guide

Table of Contents

CHAPTER ONE: Understanding Your iPhone 7

The world has become a global village where people tend to get in contact regardless of the distance between them. This is so because of the gradually advancing technology characterized by the introduction of communication gadgets that have gained control over the global business. Many companies have strived to produce different models of the communication devices. For example, the Apple, Samsung, Tecno and the Nokia companies have introduced into the market a variety of phone and accessories models to meet the different customer tastes.

Therefore, as an upgrade of the Apple handsets founded as a combined work of Steve Wozniak and Ronald Wayne in the year 1976, for example, the Apple iPhone 7 is believed to improve the important aspect of the iPhone experience by introducing the brightest and most colorful iPhone display ever. That is, the quad-core Apple 10 Fusion processor powers the iPhone 7 among several other outstanding features.

The new and outstanding iPhone model that is a single sim smartphone undergoes a 9-step anodization as well as a polishing process. This makes its surface as hard as other anodized Apple gadgets. In addition to this, the iPhone 7 and the iPhone 7 Plus comes with the several other unique features that make them excellent purchases in the current market.

The iPhone, just like most gadget, helps in a number of operations that are aimed at making the user feel the value of his or her hard-earned cash. That is, the iPhone 7 gives the user an opportunity to read his or her stored content while on the go. This is because of the small and portable size that the gadget comes in.

The iPhone 7 gadget comes in different colors to meet the different clients' interests: black, golden, white, rose gold and jet black.

To enhance your experience while using this iPhone 7, dealers have produced several user manuals to make the gadget handy. The manuals contain all the information you would desire to understand everything about the iPhone 7 gadget. This includes all the information about the special features of this iPhone 7-upgraded model. Important guides to ensure the new users find the device handy are as well included in the user guide book. The manual will provide the explanation on the preliminary activities get started with the gadget for a memorable experience.

Understanding all the properties that define this outstanding iPhone 7 is the initial step before getting your hand on the device to enjoy both the entertaining and educative content stored in the large internal storage of up to 32GB.

With all the attractive features, the iPhone 7 device comes in a reasonable price tag that matches it.

With the aim of getting the best out of this phone while on the go, therefore, it is important to access a copy of the manual, especially for the new users. This manual, just as illustrated above, includes all the information including the steps entailed before you begin enjoying the special iPhone 7 features by navigating through the touchscreen.

Do not be left out as the elites strive to maintain their class with the Apple product. Match the class of the elites, therefore, by purchasing this iPhone 7 device and enjoy the spectacular properties of the device, including the best battery life as well as the brightest and most colorful iPhone display.

To get a grip of all the features of this easy-to-use device, the next chapter will describe the specific properties to help you get the best out of the smartphone.

CHAPTER TWO: The Special Features of the iPhone 7

In an event at San Francisco in the year 2016, the Apple company introduced the new iPhone 7 and the iPhone 7 Plus. Both the handsets are characterized with unique and prestigious features that attract most of its users who endeavor to feel the value of their hard-earned money.

The Apple's new release iPhone 7 is impressive compared to the preceding models. Because of the outstanding features included, this Apple device has become the best-selling smartphone in the market for those who desire to value themselves. This chapter, therefore, presents some of the best features that characterize this classy device.

1. The design

From a distance, both the iPhone 7 and the iPhone 7 Plus smartphones have the same design as the preceding iPhone 6 and the iPhone 6 Plus. With the gadget in your hand, however, there are a number of improvements made to better the design of this valuable phone. Unlike the earlier Apple releases, for example, the antennas of this new generation device has been redesigned to be less offensive. Other than the antennas, the camera bump is curved with the continuous aluminum housing of the phone for a seamless feel and look.

iPhone 7 design

With Nokia relaunching the 3310 model, the Apple Company has also introduced the iPhone 7 Plus retro that comes in the original design of the first Apple release in the 1980's. Unlike the common iPhone 7 and the iPhone 7 Plus, this nostalgic release comes with the design that hallmarks the 80's pop culture. That is, the cover is shaded with the **retro 80's electronic beige.** The Apple logo is shaded in rainbow colors different from the normal iPhone 7 and the iPhone 7 Plus models released. This same rainbow apple logo characterized the Macintosh computer that had been released back in 1987. This is available to those who values the ancient experiences.

iPhone 7 Plus retro with a rainbow apple logo

2. The brightest and most colorful iPhone display

This is one of the major improvements made on the previous iPhone models released into the market. Both the iPhone 7 and the iPhone 7 Plus Apple models are characterized by the updated Retina HD displays that are 25% brighter than the displays from the models produced in the past years. The screens of this outstanding release support an array of colors.

Just like the previous releases, however, the screens of both the iPhone 7 and the iPhone 7 Plus as well support the memorable 3D Touch.

3. Upgraded and powerful camera

The iPhone 7 is characterized with upgraded cameras to enable it to take clear and sharper snapshots even in low-light conditions. With the 12-megapixel sensor that features in the iPhone 7, the handset becomes even 60% faster than the preceding releases. This is further enhanced by the availability of the quad-LED flashlight that has a 50% light output. With different focal length, the user of this handset is able to choose on whether to shoot photos with either the telephoto or rather the wide-angle lens.

The iPhone 7 Plus, however, comes with a new and improved dual-lens camera (two 12 mega-pixels cameras) that is much better than the iPhone 7. Using the zoom features that can zooms up to 2x for the hardware and10x for the software, therefore, the iPhone 7 Plus uses both of its 12-megapixel rear cameras for a better experience. One rear camera has a wide-angle (28mm) lens while the other one has a telephoto lens (56mm). As an advantage, however, the dual camera's setup includes a feature that creates a bokeh effect. This phone provides a live preview on the screen before taking the shot.

Both the iPhone 7 and the iPhone 7 Plus handsets include a 7 megapixel FaceTime camera for the lovers of video chats and selfies.

4. Powered by A10 chip

Both the iPhone 7 and the iPhone 7 Plus are powered by a new 64-bit quad-core chipset known as the A10 Fusion SoC. This processor comes with two high-performance cores that operate 40% faster than the initial A9 chip. Other than the two high-performance cores, the new Apple releases also include two high-efficiency cores that enhance the battery life.

The handset also includes a new 6-core GPU that is 50% faster than the Apple A9 processor of the preceding models.

This A10 Fusion chip, with an all-new four-core design, makes both the iPhone 7 and the iPhone 7 Plus to be two times faster than the preceding iPhone 6 and the iPhone 6 Plus. In addition to this, the user enjoys more time between the charges.

5. Stereo speakers

To improve the quality of the sound produced by the Apple phones, both the iPhone 7 and the iPhone 7 Plus come with two stereo speakers: one at the top while the other one at the bottom of the handset. Because of this, these 2016 releases produce two times the audio output as produced by the preceding iPhone 6 and the iPhone 6 Plus.

As a modification to this new iPhone model, the common 3.5mm audio port is replaced with the new Lightning EarPods. However, for those who still desire to listen to music or videos using their old earphones, this new model comes with an outstanding 3.5mm headphone jack adapter to ensure you enjoy the experience.

Other than the EarPod, this iPhone 7 and the iPhone 7 Plus introduces the game-changing listening experience device known as the AirPods.

6. New home button

Unlike the preceding iPhone 6 and iPhone 6 Plus, the new iPhone 7 and the iPhone 7 Plus come with many sensitive screens that use the new Topic engine for a better experience when navigating through the touch screen. The vibration-based taptic feedback system vibrates upon touching to give the users feedback.

7. Faster LTE with the best worldwide roaming

With an advanced LTE with speed of up to 450 Mbps, the device is two times faster when downloading data compared to the iPhone 6. The LTE bands introduce the best worldwide roaming to ensure you enjoy your device while on the go.

For clear and crisp sound while making calls, the iPhone 7 supports the **Voice over LTE** (VoLTE), which is a high-quality wideband calls.

A unique Wi-Fi calling option provides an easy way of making and receiving calls over the Wi-Fi connection in case the cellular service is unavailable.

Another excellent experience when it comes to calling using this iPhone 7 model is that the LTE enables the user to answer the call on applications like the Messenger, Facebook just as he or she answers the regular calls.

8. Water-resistant property

With the IP67 rating, the hardware of this iPhone 7 handset model is both water and dust-resistant. Far much advanced than the waterproofing feature by the Samsung's flagship devices, this iPhone 7 can withstand an immersion of up to 1meter depth for about 30 minutes.

With the reengineering of the entire casing, both the 2016 iPhone 7 and the iPhone 7 Plus are the first waterproof iPhones to be released into the market.

9. A 32GB internal storage

With the advanced LTE with a speed of up to 450 Mbps and two times faster when downloading data, there is a need for enough space to store the contents. Both the iPhone 7 and the iPhone 7 Plus base models come with a 32GB internal storage capacity to contain all the content you desire to have stored in your gadget.

This new iPhone release, however, comes with three variant- 32GB, 128GB (mid-tier) and the 256GB as the top tier of all the iPhones released.

With the enough space for data storage, unfortunately, there is no expandable storage for additional contents.

Now aware of the unique and important features that define the iPhone 7 and iPhone 7 Plus, it is now time to visit any iPhone dealer near you and acquire one of your own in order to enjoy the memorable experience that comes with the Apple improved reengineering.

CHAPTER THREE: Setting Up Your IPhone 7 and IPhone 7 Plus

With the iPhone 7 or the iPhone 7 Plus in your hand, there are some housekeeping details that have to be considered first in ensuring that you feel the value of your hard-earned cash. For example, it is important to activate your Apple product once you unpack it. This is the initial step before beginning the setup procedure. Before the activation, however, backing up your old handset then transfer your content into your new iPhone 7 or the iPhone 7 Plus is mandatory.

The activation involves signing in with your individual Apple ID while the gadget is connected to an active network connection. The activation process takes up to 3 minutes. To do this, there are two different methods that can be used to perform the activation procedure: iTunes Activation Method and the Wi-Fi/OTA Activation Method.

A. Turning on your iPhone 7

Immediately you unpack the gadget, press and hold the **Sleep/Wake button** until an Apple logo displays on the screen for the device. On the Home screen, slide to the right in order to continue.

B. Backing up your old phone

Before opting to use your new iPhone gadget, it is advisable to back up your old phone contents. To do this, however, connect the device to a PC then open the **iTunes**. From here, tap your device from the PC screen display (at the top left of the screen). Begin the backing up procedure to the PC. Unlike the use of OTA or rather the Wi-Fi methods, the use of the iTunes makes backup process extremely fast.

C. Upgrading the device to iOS 10.0.2

Both the iPhone 7 and the iPhone 7 Plus come with already upgraded iOS 10. It is, however, advisable for the Apple users to upgrade regularly their gadgets in case of an introduced OS upgrade by the Apple dealers. Upgrading your iPhone from time to time makes your gadget more secure than the crowding Android devices currently in the market.

To do this, connect your brand new iPhone to an active network connection and begin downloading the new update. For faster updates, however, connect your gadget to a PC. Download the update and transfer it to your phone using either the USB cable or the iTunes.

D. Restoring the backup to the new device

With an upgraded operating system, it is now time to restore the backups to your new iPhone 7. From the Set Up iPhone screen, click on the Restore Backup. In a period of 30 minutes, all data on your old phone will be transferred into the new one.

Once the process is complete, you are now free to erase the data from your old phone. To do this, therefore, tap on the **Settings** > **General** > **Reset** > **Erase All Content and Settings**.

If you do not have any backup or device, however, tap on the **Set Up as New iPhone** option and continue the setup process.

E. Activate your iPhone 7

For your new iPhone 7 to work, it has to be activated. This involves signing in with your personal Apple ID together with a password. It is, therefore, important to confirm whether the phone is activated before using it. This is done by trying to make a call or access a web when the Wi-Fi is turned off. In case either or both fail to work, access both the IMEI and the serial numbers of the iPhone. This is found by clicking the **Settings** > **General** > **About** (towards the bottom of the options displayed).

In case you forget your Apple ID or lack one, click on the **Don't have an Apple ID or forgot it** in order to recover the ID or password. From here it is also possible to create either an Apple ID or even the option to set it up later.

For the owners of multiple Apple IDs, click on the **Use different Apple IDs** for both the iCloud and the iTunes.

Once the signing in is complete, tap the **Accept** option to agree to the iOS terms and conditions and then follow the displayed steps in order to set up the Apple Pay, iCloud Keychain and the iCloud Drive.

F. Set up the Touch ID and a passcode

During the setup operations, you will be prompted to set up a **Touch ID Now** or the **Setup Touch ID Later**. The Touch ID is a feature that keeps your iPhone contents secure from unauthorized persons. The screen will always be sensitive to only your finger for unlocking anytime you need to navigate the screen of your gadget.

To set up the Touch ID, therefore, choose the **Setup Touch ID Now**. Confirm this process by clicking on the **Continue** icon.

Click on the **Setup Touch ID Later**, however, if you desire to skip this step. As well, confirm this procedure by tapping the **Continue** icon.

The next step involves creating a 6-digits password to protect further your iPhone 7 data. To do this, go to **Settings** then select **General** and then the **Passcode** option. From this Passcode option, enter your desired 6-digits passcode and then reenter the passcode before confirming the operation. To skip setting up a passcode, choose from the Passcode options **Don't Add Passcode** icon and confirm in order to skip to the next setting up procedure.

G. Set up Siri

Siri is a new feature that comes with the upgraded iOS 10. With this feature, it is possible for the user to operate the iPhone from the lock screen. Speaking phrases ensures that Siri gets to master your voice. The user is, for example, able to dial contacts from the lock screen.

To set up Siri, however, press and hold the **Home** button. Alternatively, you can click on the **Turn on Siri Later** to skip to the next setting up procedure.

To prevent intruders from using the feature in order to get access to your phone, visit the **Settings** then the **Touch ID& Passcode**. From this **Touch ID &Passcode** option, scroll down to turn off the access to Siri among other items.

H. Customize the click of your Home button

With the new and upgraded iPhone 7 and iPhone 7 Plus, it is possible to change how the Home button responds to touch. To do this, click an **option**, then the **Home** button. From here, tap **Next** in order to set your desired Home button response.

If you desire, however, to skip this setting or rather decide to change it later, click on the **Customize Later** option found when you open the **Settings**.

I. Automatic App updates

Unlike the Android phones, the new iPhone 7 and the iPhone 7 Plus new releases have the ability to automatically remove the unwanted spyware as well as the malware. With this device, therefore, it is not necessary to update the apps manually.

To set this feature, however, go to **Settings** then click the **Apps and iTunes Stores**. Once this operation is completed, the updates will automatically be downloaded. The downloading process makes use of an active network connection. This means that the user ought to turn off the Cellular data and allow the process occur when in a Wi-Fi zone.

To select the application you desire to be automatically updated, go to **Settings** then **General** and finally scroll to **Background App Refresh**. From this option, choose the item you need to update automatically. If you wish that all the apps be automatically updated, however, turn on the Background App Refresh.

J. Wi-Fi or Cellular App Connectivity

This feature gives the user an option on how his or her applications connect to the internet connection. To set this up, go to **Settings** then scroll down about four items to **Cellular**. From this point, navigate through the list of apps and turn on the applications that you allow to connect via the cellular. Turning off the app, therefore, means that the app will connect only via the Wi-Fi.

For those apps that you consider most useful and would really need to access the net. In such a case, turn on both the cellular and the Wi-Fi internet connection.

K. Wi-Fi Calling feature

To make calls, you need to purchase sufficient calling cards. With your iPhone 7 or the iPhone 7 Plus, however, a Wi-Fi calling feature accompanies it to make you avoid the inconveniences of inadequate airtime to make important and urgent calls.

With this feature, your calls come through when the device is connected to an active Wi-Fi internet connection. To set this, visit the **Settings** option then select the **Phone** and then the **Wi-Fi Calling** option. From this point, you can turn on the feature and enjoy it as you wish. During the turning on of this feature, the user is prompted to enter his or her emergency address (address from where he or she will be using the Wi-Fi calling).

L. App developer and display resolution

The iPhone 7 and the iPhone 7 Plus handsets come with outstanding app developers that give the user the power to decide whether to share their information or not.

Depending on the vision of the users, both the Apple latest releases come with an option of choosing the display resolution a user finds convenient with him or her. That is, the standard resolution (this displays more on the screen) and the zoomed display that uses larger text fonts. To enable this, go to **Settings** then select your desired view option. Once this is done, click on **Next** icon to proceed to enjoy your device.

M. Finish your iPhone setup process

Once all the features are up-to-date, click on the displayed **Get Started** option to enjoy the device.

To keep copies of your contents for conveniences, it is advisable for the user to back up his or her data.

With the features explained in this chapter, the new users will find it easy to make good use of their excellent buy.

CHAPTER FOUR: Managing Your iPhone 7 Contents and Applications

With the large storage space in iPhone 7 and iPhone 7 Plus, managing the hundreds of files, apps, and documents requires effective mechanisms that introduce a new and memorable experience for the user during the data managing session.

To look into this, the newly released iPhone 7 and the iPhone 7 Plus gadgets introduces new applications that are meant for the organization of your files according to your taste.

In addition to the files being organized, the file manager allows effective synchronizing as well as sharing items across devices.

A. File Manager (Free)

With this app in your iPhone gadget, it is easy to organize your files in an aesthetical manner. This file manager application is available for both the iPhone and iPad with an in-app purchase to upgrade from the App Store. With the ability to synchronize with multiple clouds support such as the OneDrive, Dropbox, the data management becomes so effective. Because of this file manager app, the user is able to access his or her data any time he or she feels convenient.

The app also includes an integrated music player as well as a PDF reader for comfortable and convenient listening to music and reading of the PDF files respectively. To make it even outstanding, this iPhone and the iPad app support the Microsoft Office, Excel as well as the PowerPoint for easy access to the different content formats.

Because of the ability to transfer the files from the Mac or computer to your iPhone 7 with efficiency, this File Manager (Free) can as well be called a virtual USB drive.

A built-in search feature makes it effective for the user to search for the data he or she intends to access as fast as possible.

To manage the files in a convenient and smart manner, you can use this file manager application to sort the content by either the name, date, kind or size of the file.

B. The Document 5

Other than the file manager (Free), Document 5 is another outstanding file management app to help you in organizing your iPhone content to match your class.

Just like the File Manager (Free), this Document 5 app synchronizes with the cloud services like the iCloud, OneDrive, Google Drive as well as the Dropbox for effective file management.

Other than the ability to upload and share files from this file manager app, the media player makes it convenient for the videos and music as well as a built-in viewer to display the photos among other files of the like.

Downloading of the articles, including the annotate PDF documents and saving them for future reading is enabled using this file manager app.

With a password protection feature, it is possible to set your preferred passcode to protect your content from unauthorized individuals.

C. FileApp

Just like the other file managers, this FileApp is an effective data manager that allows the user to play the multimedia contents.

This app makes it possible for the user to enjoy the privileges by the lovers of the Windows Explorer of the Finder found on the Mac of storing the important iOS files as well as the folders in your iPhone.

You can as well design the photos in this file manager as you wish due to the built-in image editor. Once edited, the user can make use of the slideshow feature to view his or her photos. Multiple images, as well as other stored files, can be sent via the email as attachments or instantly share them via Facebook and Twitter.

Besides setting the privacy passcode or the wireless transfer password, considering a file encryption with the iOS data protection, the user effectively secures his or her files from unauthorized personalities.

D. iFiles

The file manager can synchronize with all the cloud services like the Dropbox, Google Drive among others for effective iPhone content management.

The Web downloader feature included in the iFiles file manager allows you to download content from the internet into your iPhone gadget, not to forget the PDF viewer that allows the user to read the contents that are in PDF formats.

This file manager app available in the App Store includes other features such as the clipboard paste option, voice recorder, photo import, media player as well as zip and extract capabilities. This ensures that the user has total control over his or her iPhone gadget.

E. FileMaster

This outstanding file manager able to work on either your iPhone, iPod touch as well as the iPad allows the user to organize his or her files in a smart and convenient manner. That is the documents, music, photos and videos. Just like the other file manager apps, FileMaster syncs with the iPhone cloud services like the Dropbox among the others.

A password protection, as well as the ability to hide your desired files and folders, are nice features that ensure that your files are inaccessible to the unauthorized persons.

Both the built-in media player and the photo import features enhance your file management experience. Sharing and transferring of the files in this app is also possible.

F. File Manager Pro App

This file organization solution is effective for all the Apple documents, Office files, audio, photos, PDFs, and the videos.

With this app, the user is able to create as well as mark contents either as print documents, zip or extract files or favorites. To make it even better, it is possible to share the files via the email.

The app also has the ability to synchronize with the cloud services such as the Dropbox, SkyDrive among the others.

Opening documents from other apps or email are possible while using this app.

This app available in the App Store has a password protection features that allows the user to secure his or her downloads using the Web download feature.

G. istorage 2HD

With this app, the user is able to view as well as manage his or her files in a more organized manner.

Considered an excellent code editor, the users have the chance to enjoy the editing sessions as well as transferring multiple data at the same time.

The user can save files, including the protected PDF, Rar and ZIP files, on his or her iPhone gadget for reading at his or her own convenience.

The included built-in browser allows the user to, in addition to accessing the web files, save the files directly from the web into his or her iPhone.

For a file manager with built-in storage space or just able to sync with a current cloud service you are using, consider one file manager whose features interest you.

For the Windows users, however, the files can only be accessed through the SMB protocol. In the presence of an active internet connection, simply drag-drop from Mac to your iPhone. This app as well synchronizes with the cloud services like the Dropbox.

Managing the memory and the expansion of storage space

iPhone 7 comes with large built-in storage capacity to provide enough space for your items, including the unique and powerful features that come with the new Apple release.

The handset, however, does not provide a micro SD support limiting the users' desire to expand their storage space. It is for this reason that high-storage capacity iPhone 7 models were as well introduced (128GB and 256GB iPhone 7 versions).

Regardless of the higher built-in storage, various factors such as the extensive usage, processes, and apps among other. For example, an extended period of using your handset fills its memory with processes and hence slowing down the performance of the gadget.

In addition to the slowing down effects, lack of enough memory hinders the upgrading to new iOS, downloading apps as well as backing up contents.

To boost the general phone performance. Therefore, it is advisable to free up your iPhone storage space. iPhone 7 comes with a PhoneClean app that helps in the removal of useless files, caches among other junks to help automatically free the gadget storage space.

Other than the smart iPhone-cleaning tool, many different ways can be used to manage the handset's storage capacity.

1. Check the iPhone storage

In the case of a slowed iPhone performance, there is need to confirm the applications or items that use much of your iPhone's internal storage space. This allows you to determine also the amount of space that is left on your gadget. To do this, two different ways can be applicable:

a. Check and manage the memory from the Settings menu

➤ From the **Home screen**, tap the **Settings** then scroll to **General** and click on it.

➤ From here, click on the **Storage & icloud Usage** to continue. After this, you should be able to see your storage details, including both the used and the remaining spaces.

- ➤ Click on the **Manage Storage** in order to view the list of all the apps and the size of each one of them.
- ➤ Tap on the app to display the app's memory. This provides the option to delete some of the contents depending on the application.

In occasions when you are prompted with a **Storage Almost Full** alert, it is advisable to remove any unnecessary contents from your iPhone gadget for improved performance.

b. **Using iTunes to check and manage your memory**

- ➤ To do this, your device must be connected to a computer with an installed iTunes app.
- ➤ From your computer, click to open the iTunes
- ➤ Connect your device via a USB cable to the computer
- ➤ From the iTunes, identify your device and click on it. This displays the memory details as well as the iOS content uses, divided by the content type
- ➤ Move your mouse over a content type to see more information on **Other** or **Apps**, for example.

2. Use a soft reset to clear your iPhone internal memory

With the lack of built-in RAM management options within the iOS, a simple reboot or soft reset can help to clear the RAM. To do this, press and hold the **Sleep/Wake** button until prompted to power off your device. After about 30 seconds, press and hold the **Sleep/Wake** button once again until the Apple logo shows up.

3. Updating your iPhone 7 software

To maintain your device in a stable state, it is advisable to update your iPhone iOS. To identify any software updates for your iPhone 7, visit the **Settings** > **General** > **Software Update**.

In the case of any update for performance improvement, therefore, simply follow a prompt to download and install the software update for your iPhone 7.

4. Backing up big files

File such as the songs, photos, and videos take much of the available space. To free memory for better performance, back up the files to other storage destinations such as the Cloud, hard drive, computer among others before removing them from your device to create more space for excellent performance.

5. Clearing of history, attachment, and cache

During the checking up of the memory details, you may decide to clear the chatting history, attachments as well as cached files. To make it even easier, some apps offer the users a way to clear its cache and history. For example, to clean all the Safari app history and data, go to **Settings** > **Safari** > **Clear History and Website Data**.

CHAPTER FIVE: Performing the Common Troubleshooting Solutions

Since the introduction of iPhone 7 into the market, users have enjoyed the improved experience that comes with it.

Some issues, however, hinder the owners of these iPhone gadgets from enjoying the fun. To curb this, the Apple Company has filtered feedbacks from the global users in order to mitigate the most common issues that have been reported since the release of this device.

This chapter, therefore, provides the common issues and potential fixes to get your smile back.

A. Hissing sound made by the iPhone 7

Most of the iPhone 7 users have complained of a mysterious hissing sound that comes from the back of the gadget near the Apple logo. This sound seems louder when the Apple product is under heavy load. The problem has brought many controversies with dealers giving varying claims that the noise is due to the "coil whine" that comes from the A10 Fusion chip. Others claim that this problem arises because of interference with the speaker system or due to the RF transmitter.

Solution

Currently, there is no effective way to rectify this internal hardware problem. Not all the iPhone 7 and iPhone 7 Plus have the problem, and hence it is advisable to visit any Apple Store and replace it with a new one.

B. Poor battery life

Because of the introduction of the A10 Fusion chip, iPhone 7 is the best Apple release when it comes to lasting battery life.

However, many cases of battery drain have been reported especially for those with the updated iOS 10.2.

Solution

Similar to the irritating hissing sound, this poor battery life has no solid fix and depend greatly on the usage pattern of the user.

Turning to Low Power Mode is a way to minimize the draining of the battery life. To do this, go to **Settings** then scroll to **Battery** and then turn on the **Low Power Mode** to ensure a longer battery life between the charges.

Another way to control the draining is to manage the apps that consumes much power. To conduct this, visit **Battery Usage** found in the **Settings**. From here scroll down to **Battery** and identify the app that interferes with the quality of the battery.

C. Poor speaker and phone call quality

Another problem that most users have raised in their reviews is the fact that incoming audio is too low to hear.

Solution

Apple Company has updated a support forum in order to help them rectify the sound concern. For example, the following interventions have been recommended to help curb this sound issue:

1) In the case of the occurrence of this issue, go to **Settings** then scroll to **Sounds**. From the Sounds, drag both the Alerts and Ringer sliders to increase the volume of the device.
2) For those who are able to get audio out of the speaker there are a number of strategies that can be considered to harmonize the situation:
   o Confirm that the iPhone case is not blocking the speaker.
   o Check the Ring/Silent switch on the side of the phone to confirm it is not set to Silent (Orange).
   o Restart your device.
   o Clean off any dirt, debris or dust that might be blocking the speaker.
   o Install an audio player app or the sound effects and use the volume keys or the Control Center controls to adjust the volume.
3) In case there is no change after engaging in all the rectifying strategies, it is advisable to contact the Apple Support for guidance on how to restore your smile.

D. Non-functional 3D Touch haptic feedback

With this issue, there is no feedback from the phone to indicate that the 3D was used. Just like in the preceding models, this problem has persisted into the new model with iOS 10.2.

Solutions

Despite the notice that nothing can be done to fix this error, there are a few strategies to try before disposing of your excellent iPhone handset. For example, restarting the phone has been proved to restore the 3D haptic feedback temporarily.

Other than restarting the phone to continue enjoying the outstanding 3D feature, there are a number of other potential interventions.

- ❖ Try turning off and on the System Haptic. To do this, go to **Settings** then scroll to **Sounds & Haptics**. From here, turn off the System Haptics off and the on again.
- ❖ Try adjusting the sensitivity. Go to **Settings** then **Accessibility** then taps the **3D Touch** option to turn it on and off.
- ❖ Uninstalling some apps have helped in the management of this issue. For example, it has been found that by disabling Skype integration option, your iPhone restores its memorable feature.

E. "No Service" after disabling the Airplane Mode

When traveling by air, for example, it is advisable to switch off your electronic gadgets or turn them to flight modes. After landing from the plane, most users have complained that their device displayed the "No Service" even upon disabling the Airplane Mode.

Solutions

Apple Company has not yet figured a remedy for this problem. Try, however, the following recommendations by long-term clients of the Apple products.

- ❖ Remove the SIM card from its slot and then re-insert it back and turn on the device.
- ❖ A hard reset can help the iPhone restore its original desirable state.

F. Bluetooth Connectivity Problems

Bluetooth connectivity is another problem that has been reported by most users of this Apple item. This makes it difficult to receive items from another device with an active Bluetooth or to listen to music from another Bluetooth device.

Solution

The only remedy to this problem is to "forget" the device then reconnect it. To do this, go to **Settings** then trace the **Bluetooth**. By turning on the **Bluetooth**, find the device you are finding difficulty connect with and click on the **blue "I" button** next to it. Click on the "**Forget This Device**" and then try connecting to the device again.

Resetting your network settings can be helpful when the problem persists. To do this, visit the **Settings** then click on the **General**. From here, select the **Reset** icon and finally the **Reset Network Settings**.

G. Phone approaches and freezes

A number of iPhone 7 users have complained that the Phone app either lock up or crashes when making calls using the Bluetooth headset, for example.

To manage this, the users have tried both the hard and soft as well factory reset in vain.

Solutions

The first and more reliable step to managing this condition is to update to iOS 10.2.1

The crash might have occurred immediately after an update. This can mean that the update has installed incorrectly. To deal with this, therefore, restore the device to a backup made before the update and reinstall the update.

Turning off the Exchange contacts has also been hinted to help in managing this problem. To do this, go to **Settings** > **Contacts** > **Accounts**, then click on your **Exchange account(s)** and switch the Contacts off.

There are many problems that might disrupt your experience when using both the iPhone 7 and the iPhone 7 Plus latest releases. In case you are not able to rectify the error, contact the Apple Support or rather visit any nearby Apple Store for help.

CHAPTER SIX: Hidden Tips and Tricks for a Valuable iPhone 7

iPhone 7 is a valuable purchase with outstanding features that improve the experience of users. To get the best out of the device, this chapter discusses some of the most useful iPhone 7 tips and tricks.

Among the tricks illustrated are the hidden shortcuts, iPhone keyboard tips and the iPhone tricks that most iPhone users do not know about.

1. Shaking and undo deleted Mail

With the aim of managing your iPhone 7 device, you may have accidentally archived or trashed an important email and hence the need to undo the deleted item.

To do this, hold your device tight and then shake it to pop the "undo" feature.

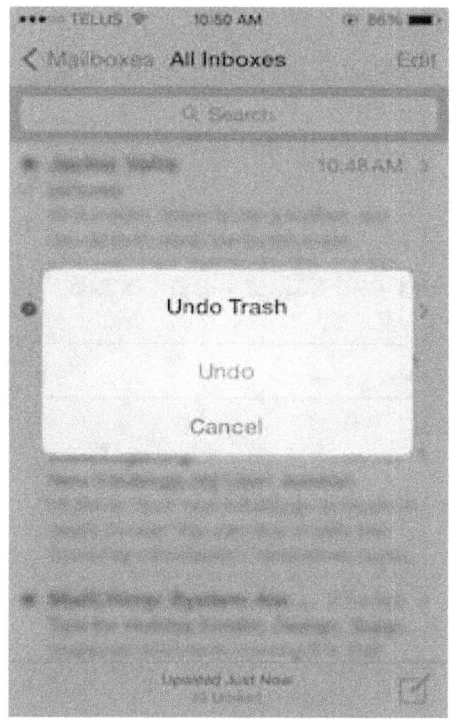

"Undo" feature after shaking your iPhone

2. Drag and drop calendar events

To save much of your time, you may need to reschedule your appointments. That is, you will need to move the calendar events around.

To move an event, therefore, simply press and hold the event and then move it up, down, right or left to change the event schedule.

3. Grabbing the .ca, .com among other extensions quickly

Sometimes typing an address can be tiresome, particularly in the case of a long address. With the iPhone 7, however, it is possible to get the most popular extensions without much struggle.

To do this, simply press and hold on the period displayed on the keyboard to reveal the extensions. From the display, the user can select the extension he or she needs.

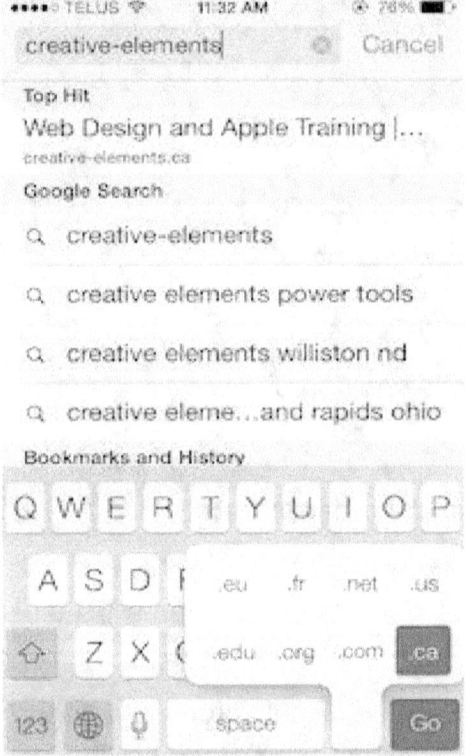

Popular extensions displayed

4. Customizing vibrations for specific contacts

With the new iPhone 7, you have the capability of predicting who is calling or rather sending a text message without having to look at the phone.

To enable this, select a contact from **Contacts** and then click on **Edit** then scroll to the **Vibrate** option in order to either choose one vibration or rather create a new one for yourself.

5. Blocking numbers

Basing on my personal experience, some callers can be so nagging and hence the feeling to limit the interaction with them.

To do this, Press the **information icon ("i")** located near the number you wish to block. Scroll down the options and tap the **Block this caller**. This prevents the imposters from disturbing you.

6. Background App Refresh

With the desire to save your iPhone battery life, there are many tips that have been recommended by the long-term Apple users or the dealers. Turning off the automatic apps refreshing will also help a great deal.

To do this, go to **Settings** then select the **General** and finally the **Background App Refresh**. Once here, turn it off in order to enhance your battery life.

7. Quitting an app

For some reasons such as controlling the energy usage by your device, it is advisable to quit some of the apps that consumes much power and hence reducing the battery life.

Unlike the case in the preceding iPhone 6, iPhone 5 and others that entailed double pressing the **Home** button then press and hold the app until the *red minus sign displays*, therefore, iOS 7 requires the user to double tap the **Home** button ad simply flick up any application he or she would wish to delete.

8. Camera flash alert

This feature allows the iPhone to flash in case of an incoming alert or rather use it as a stroboscope for your next party.

To enable this, simply go to **Settings** then tap on the **Accessibility** and finally click on the **LED Flash for Alerts**.

9. Using an iPhone 7's Volume Up Button to take photos and videos

With the new iPhone 7, it is easy to take photos and videos with convenience.

To do this, simply click **Volume up** button located on the remote on your Apple while in a camera mode.

While in the video mode, however, use the middle button (play/pause) to take selfie

10. Stopping Music with Clock

This feature automatically stops music playback after sometimes. This is convenient for those users who would wish to fall asleep to music.

To activate this property, go to **Clock** then click on **Timer** to set your desired duration. Once the duration is set, select on the **"Stop Playing" When Timer Ends**.

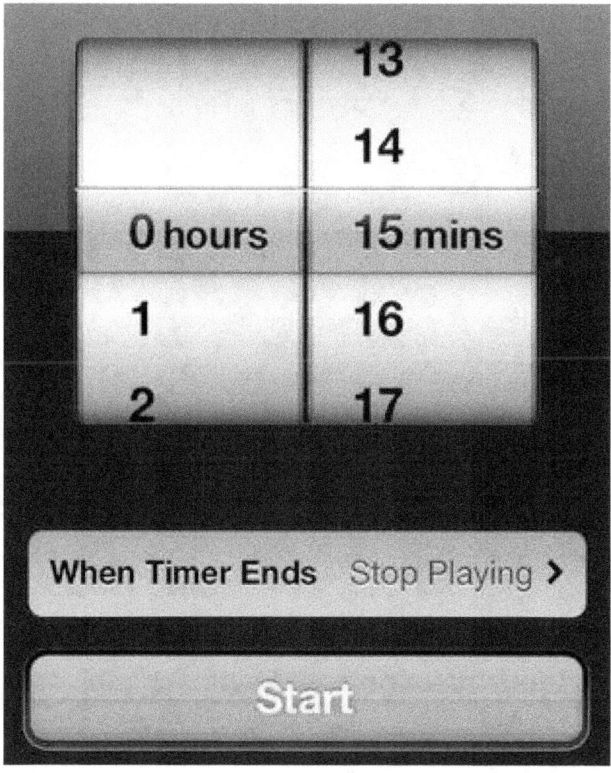

11. Assistive Touch

In the case of a broken Home button or rather having trouble touching the screen, enabling this assistive touch will help a great deal. This feature is enabled from the Accessibility settings. Once enabled a big white dot displays on the screen.

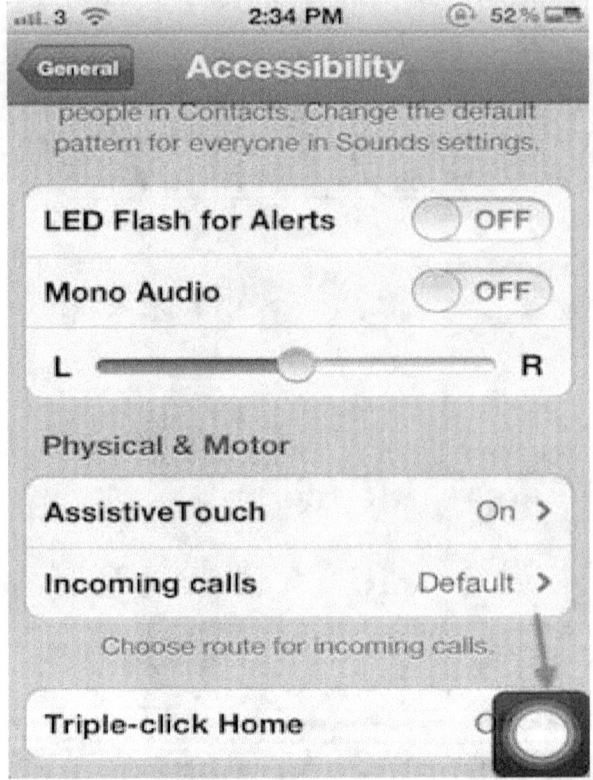

A big white dot on the screen

12. "Shortcuts" section as a keyboard trick

This feature is vital for the complicated words that will challenge you when typing. Such words can include complicated email signatures, difficult words and often-misspelled words among several others. The shortcuts teach your iPhone 7 some permanent shortcuts.

To set this go to **Settings** > **General** > **Keyboard** > **Shortcut**.

13. Permanently Switching the Caps Lock

This trick is convenient for the users who desire to write a sentence or rather an abbreviation with uppercase letters, for example. To do this, double tap to toggle the Caps Lock permanently.

14. Holding 0 to get a Degree Icon

Either it is usually discouraging when typing a chemistry or weather related text using your handset. When in need of the "degree" icon during your typing, therefore, hold the number zero for seconds until the degree icon displays above.

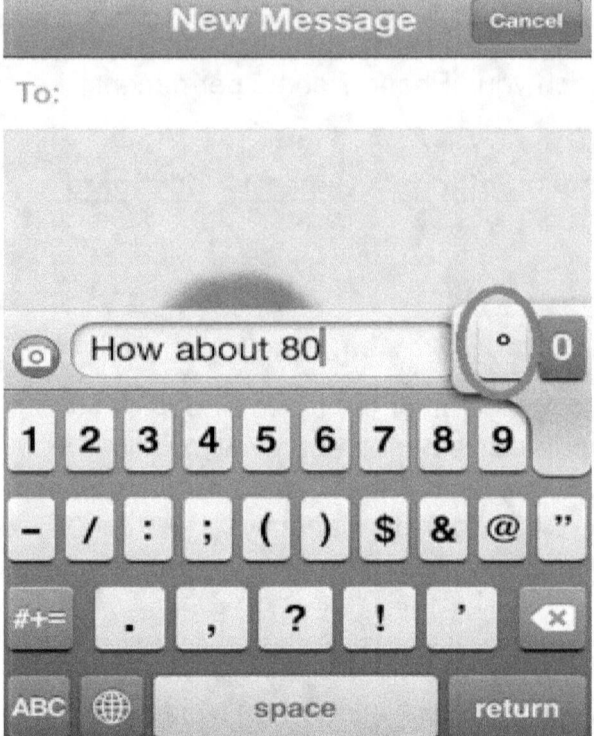

Holding the 0 to display the "degree" icon.

15. Shake to undo typing

You may want to delete a message after typing with the Keyboard. Tapping, therefore, the "delete" button one by one can be very tiresome and time-consuming.

With the new iPhone 7 release, however, a one-time shake and then selecting the **<u>Undo Typing</u>** option will ensure that all the messages are automatically deleted.

The Undo Typing option after shaking

16. Shift from Camera to Photo

When using the camera application, it is possible to
swipe from left to right, with the iPhone 7, to quickly
access photos. This is convenient that the normal
tapping on the Camera Roll thumbnail located in the
lower left.

CHAPTER SEVEN: Maintenance Information for Your IPHONE 7

To have a taste of the memorable experience that comes with using the iPhone 7, the earlier chapters of this book have provided information that is helpful to the new users. This chapter, however, specifically highlights the maintenance procedures that can ensure that your device lasts longer than you even expect.

Taking great concern on the information, herein, will ensure that you do feel the value that comes with your hard-earned cash.

A. Regular servicing of your iPhone 7

Servicing your iPhone minimizes the common issues that are reported by most users. Apple products come with a one-year warranty for free servicing and repairing in the cases of problems resulting from workmanship, for example. However, there are some of the problems that are not covered by the warranty. For example, the battery, scratches or dents, normal wear and tear as well as the device being stolen.

For technical support from Apple regarding your gadget, make an appointment to visit the nearest Apple Store.

B. Enhancing the battery health

Earlier in the book, special features that have made iPhone 7 the best choice is the fact that it comes with a prolonged battery life.

You will not be able to explore the beauty and class of this product when the phone is off and hence the need to ensure the iPhone lasts the whole day.

Controlling the way a battery is charged is a way of boosting its health. For example, ensuring that the battery charge to 100%.

Emptying the battery completely every month is also a way of prolonging the battery lifespan of the iPhone 7 and the iPhone 7 Plus.

C. Conduct a regular backup for your iPhone 7/7Plus

It sometimes hurt to lose some of your important items such as the emails and contacts in case of a failed iOS upgrade or mistaken deletion.

Backing up your content will make it easy for you to restore your lost content. Because of this, therefore, it is important to back up your iPhone 7 with either the iTunes or iCloud to avoid the inconveniences.

D. Deleting the unwanted items to improve the performance of your device

Like mentioned in the fourth chapter of this book, having the unwanted content fill the limited 32GB storage space will slow the functioning of your iPhone 7 device.

Regular monitoring of the storage memory and cleaning off the unwanted apps among other files will ensure your valuable handset operates faster at all times.

To avoid losing extremely important contents of your device, an initial backing up of your iPhone 7/7 Plus is advisable just in case you would desire to restore them back in the future.

E. Regular updating the iOS and the Apps

Apple Company releases updates that are useful in fixing a number of bugs that might hinder you from enjoying the experience of using the latest iPhone release. In addition to this, the regular updates introduces several other outstanding features for the benefit of the users. Follow the steps involved in updating your gadget, included in the fourth chapter of this publication.

Updating the apps as well improves the operation speed of the handset. To do this, visit the App Store and update the apps from here.

F. Regular restarting of the iPhone

It was noted that restarting your gadget helps in rectifying some common issues that might lower the quality of experience with your iPhone 7.

However, regular restarting of the handset, regardless of a noted issue, is an efficient way of ensuring you maintain your gadget in good shape for a longer time. The speed of the device is as well rejuvenated.

G. Purchase a screen protector as well as a case

Because of the delicate material that is used to design the iPhone handsets, a simple drop may adversely damage your device.

Regardless of the high-quality scratch-resistant screen that iOS devices features, it is advisable for the users to purchase a quality screen protector. A reliable and quality casing will act as a shock absorber in case of a drop and hence minimizes the impact of the fall.

H. Cleaning your iPhone 7 handset

The iPhone 7 release is believed to be dust-proof. Extreme mismanagement, however, will require that the user wipes the gadget to maintain its aesthetic value.

To do this, use a soft and clean clothing to avoid leaving unpleasant scratches when using abrasive materials.

I. Other maintenance procedure for your iPhone 7

Other than the maintenance above tips highlighted above, there are several other important tips to help you enhance the quality of your purchase.

For example, avoiding using the iPhone in extreme hot or cold condition is a way of enhancing its workability.

For repair or any inquiry on proper management of your iPhone 7 /7 Plus, make an appointment at any Apple Store near you.

<u>Conclusion</u>

Back in 2014, iPhone 6 (manufactured by the Apple Company) was branded a successful product release since it performed best in the market.

Two years down the line, a next-generation iPhone 7 was introduced into the market and has attracted more attention from the iPhone lovers globally. Although this iPhone 7 features a similar design as the iPhone 6, it comes with substantial upgrades compared to the preceding iPhone 6 Apple release making it an ideal buy for the Apple product lovers.

The chapters of this book include information that is helpful to the users (more specifically the new users) in order to feel the value of their purchase. That is, the features that make the iPhone 7 different from the iPhone 6, timesaving tricks when using the device, procedures for setting it up before using and tips on proper management of your iPhone 7 contents.

The book has also highlighted some of the common issue reported by the loyal users of this iPhone 7 product and steps to rectify the problems to enhance further the experience of new users.

Proper tips on the maintenance of your iPhone 7 device ensure that you enjoy the memorable experience of using the iPhone 7 gadget for a longer period without the regrets of wasting your money.

Obtain, therefore, a copy of this special guideline on how to increase the number of days to enjoy the outstanding experience that comes with the iPhone 7/7 Plus.

Finally, if you enjoyed this book, please take the time to share your thoughts and post a review on Amazon. It would be greatly appreciated! Thank you and good luck!